Instrumentals

FOR EASY PIANO

Cherry Lane Music Company
Director of Publications/Project Editor: Mark Phillips

ISBN 978-160378-357-6

Visit our website at www.cherrylaneprint.com

Alley Cat

By Frank Bjorn

Moderately, in 2

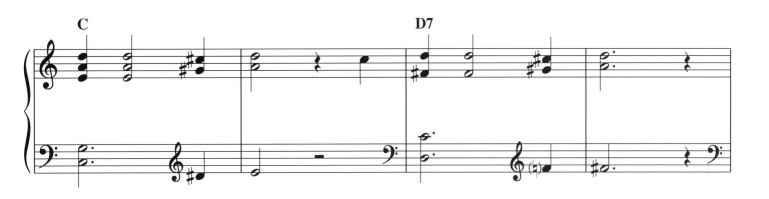

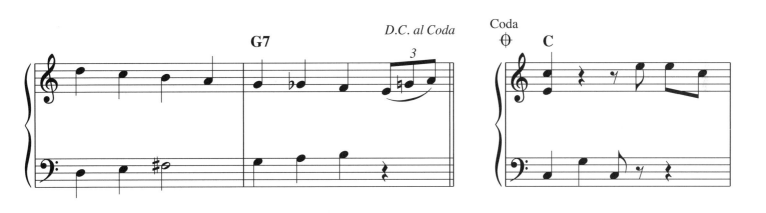

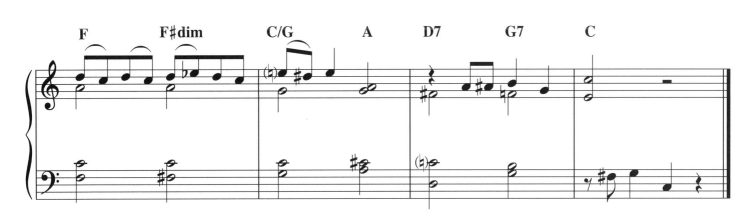

Baby Elephant Walk

from the Paramount Picture HATARI!

Words by Hal David

Music by Henry Mancini

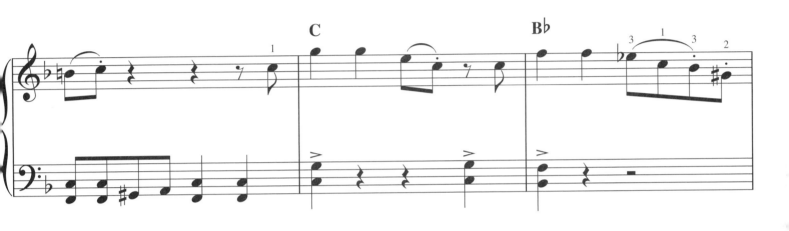

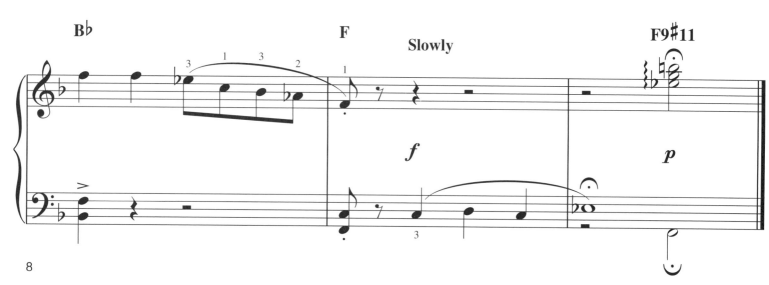

Bonanza

Theme from the TV Series

Words and Music by
Jay Livingston and Ray Evans

Medium tempo

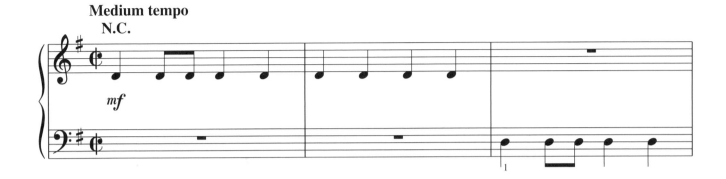

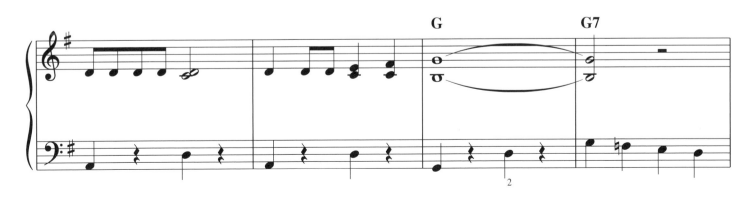

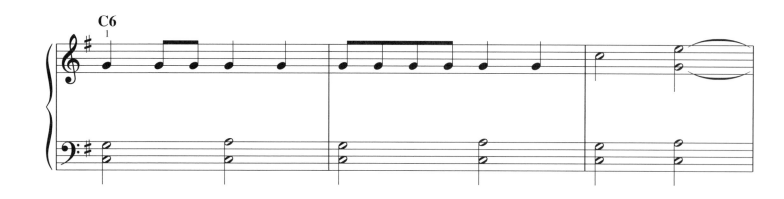

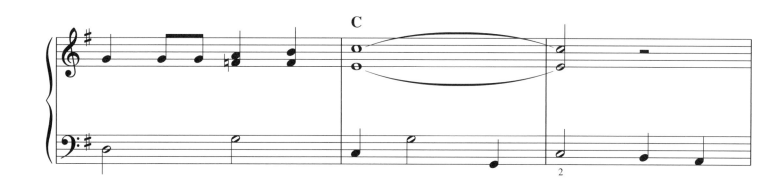

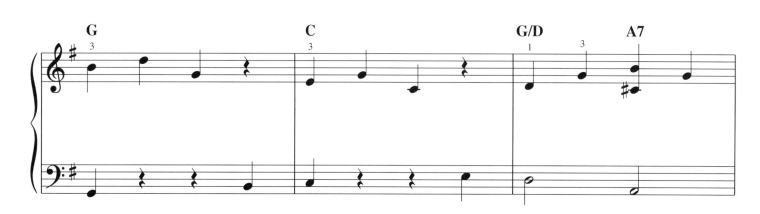

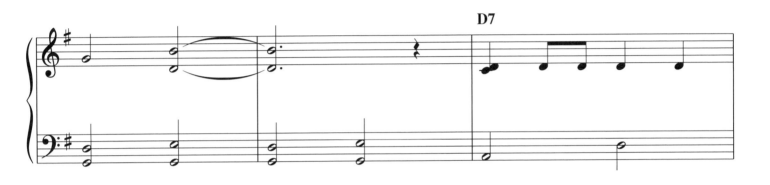

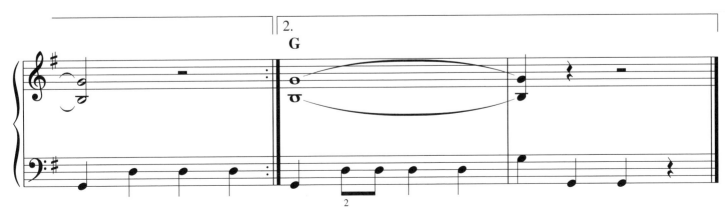

Cast Your Fate to the Wind

Music by Vince Guaraldi
Arranged by Tom Roed

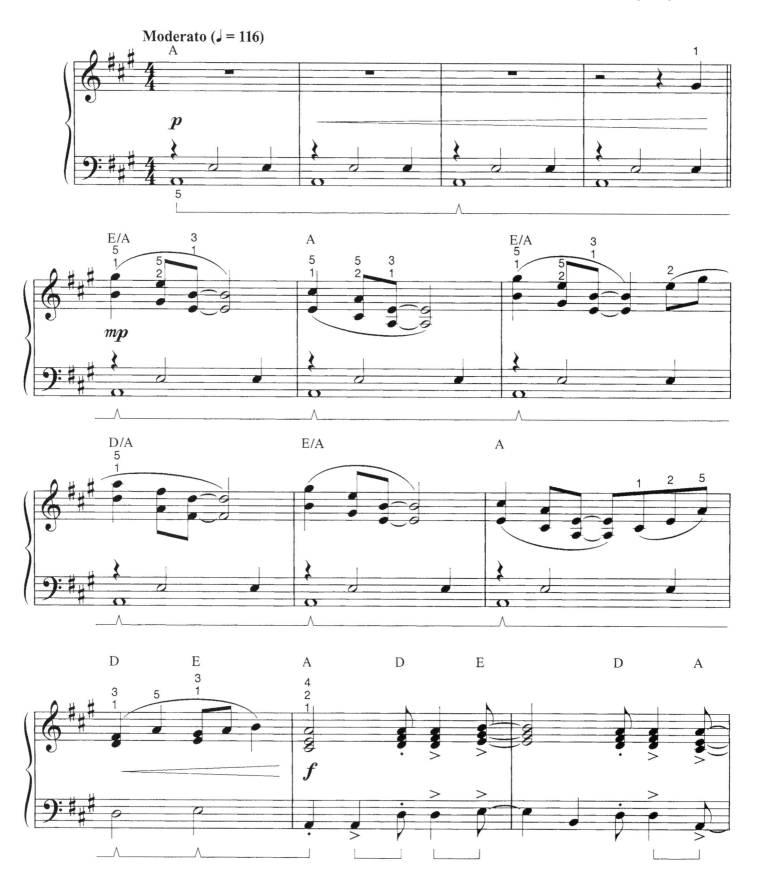

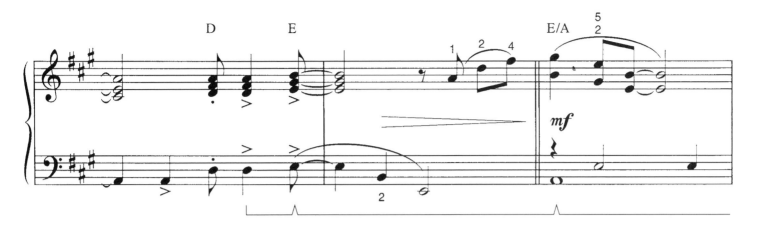

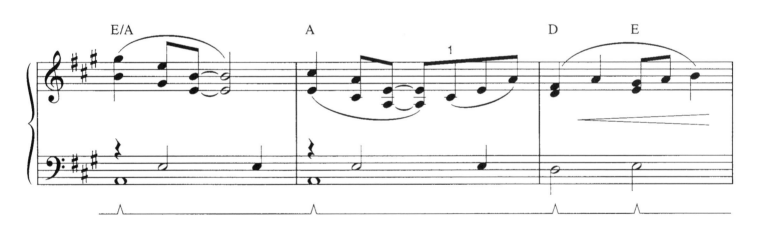

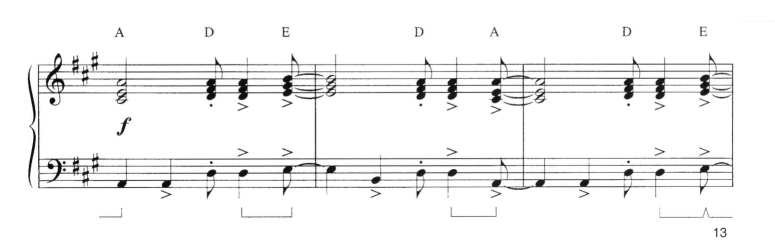

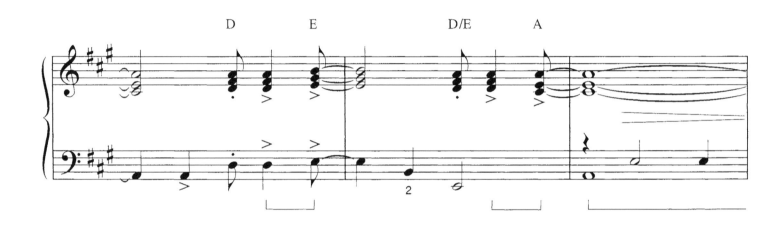

Chariots of Fire

from CHARIOTS OF FIRE

Music by Vangelis

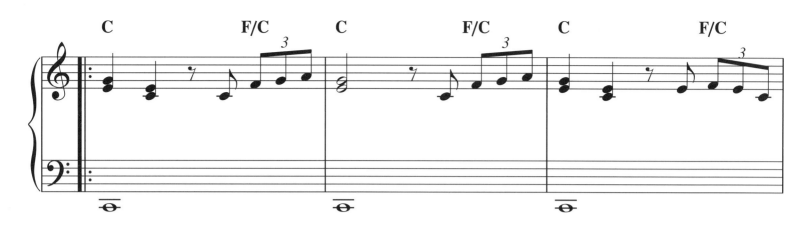

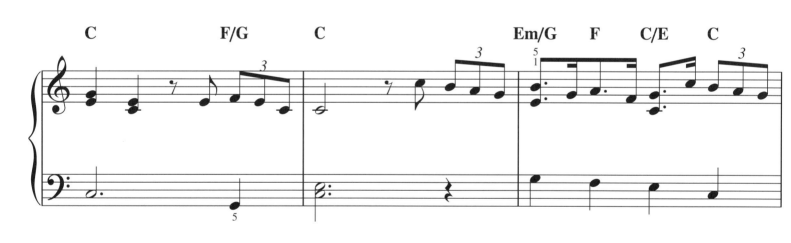

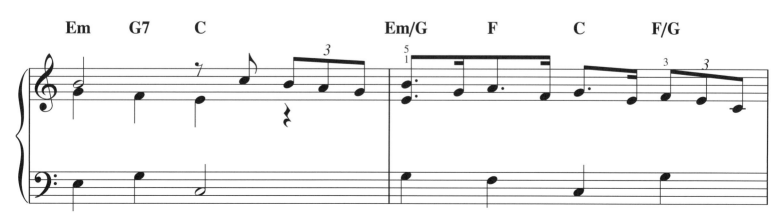

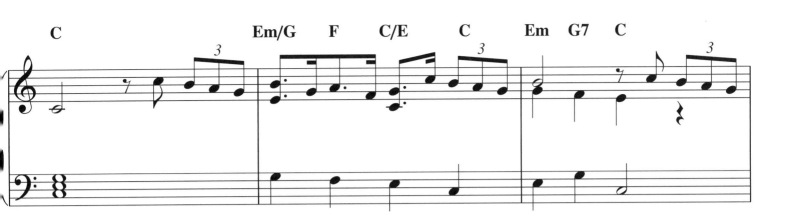

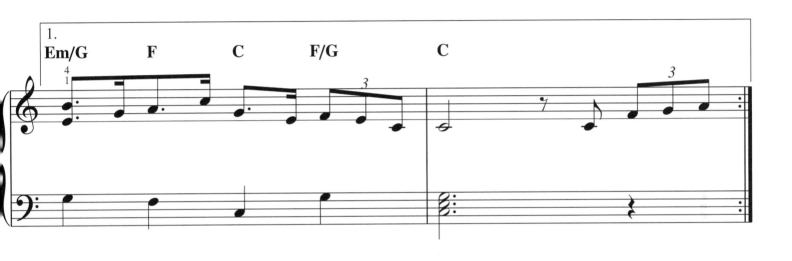

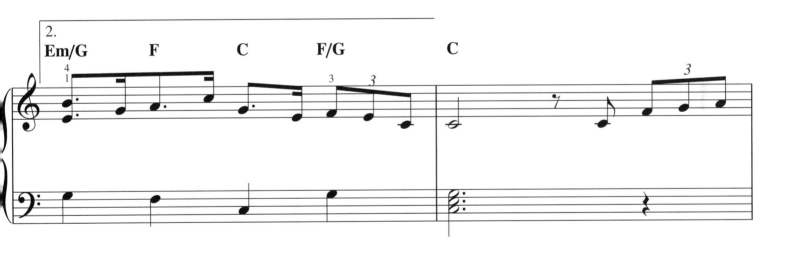

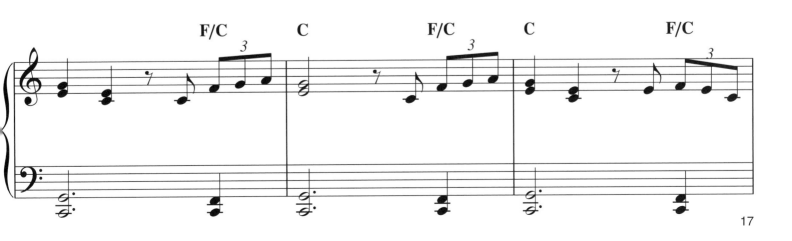

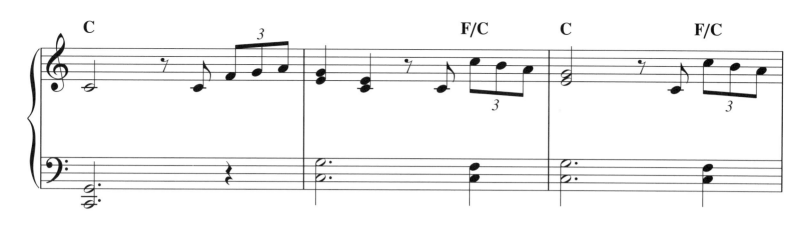

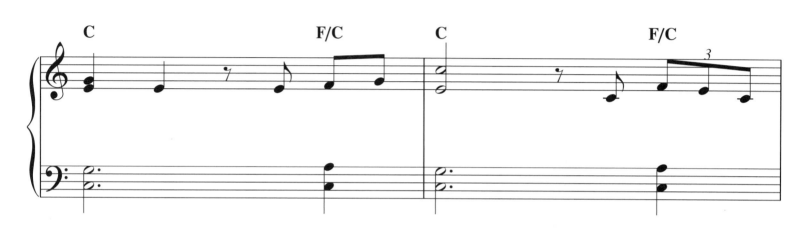

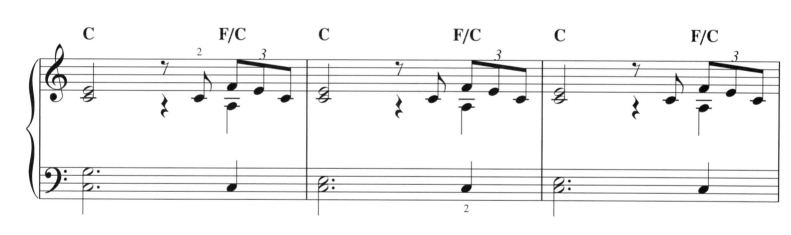

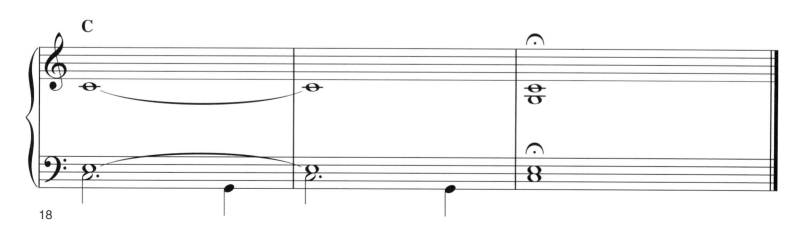

Theme from E.T.
(The Extra-Terrestrial)
from the Universal Picture E.T. (THE EXTRA-TERRESTRIAL)

Music by John Williams

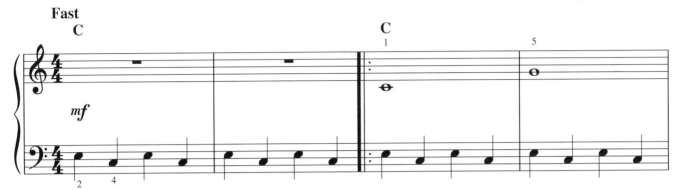

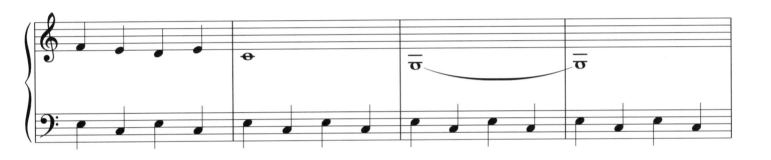

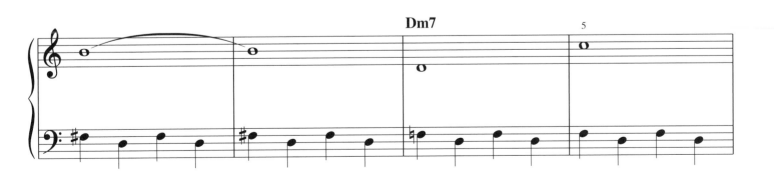

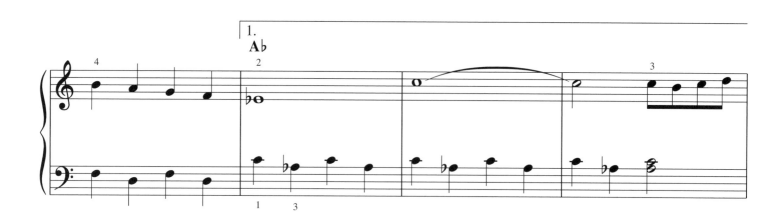

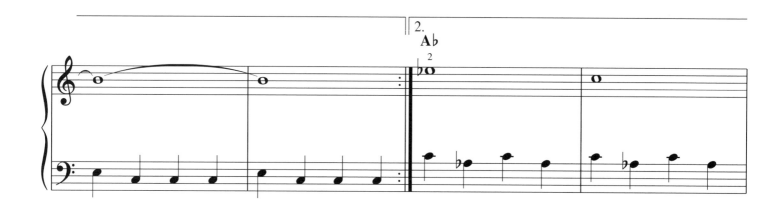

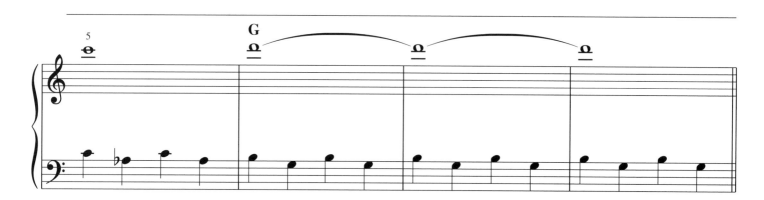

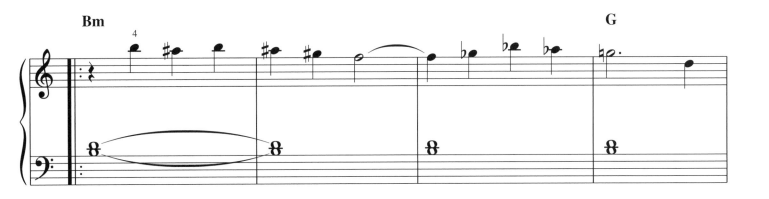

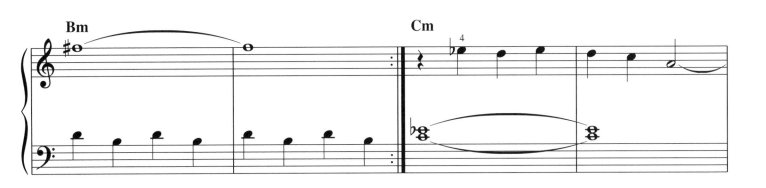

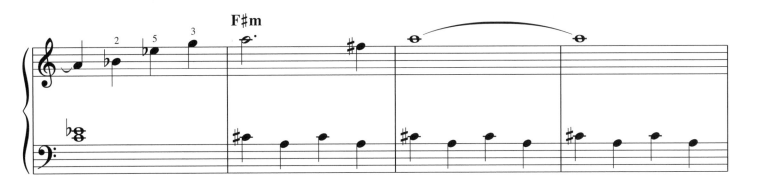

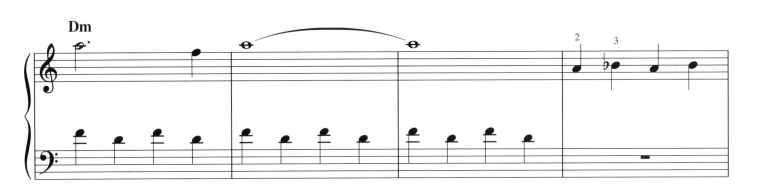

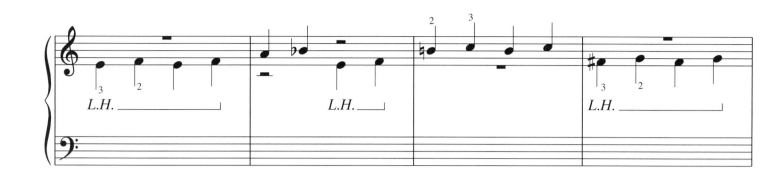

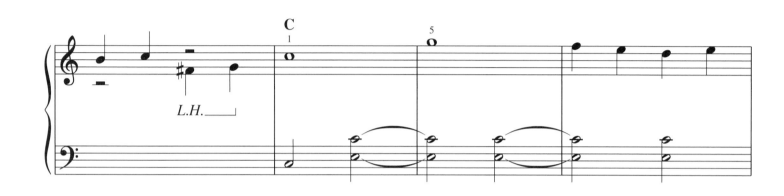

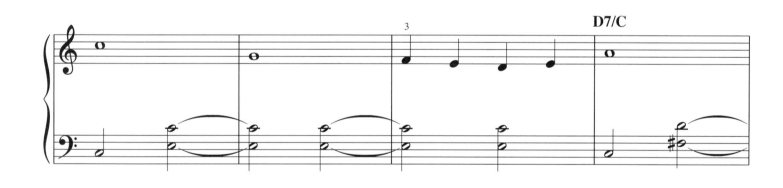

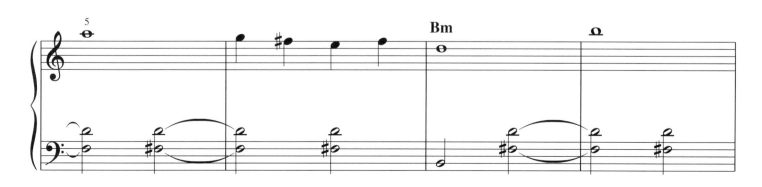

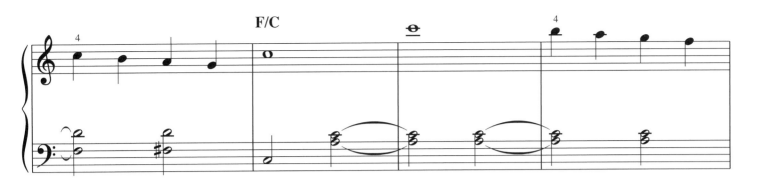

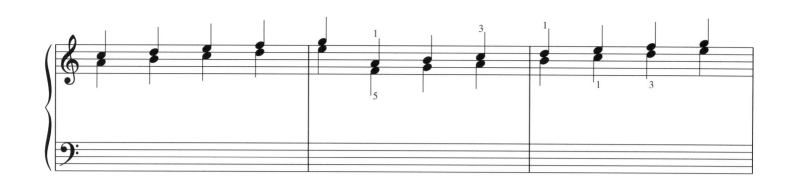

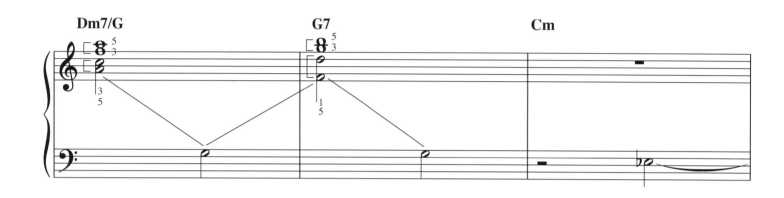

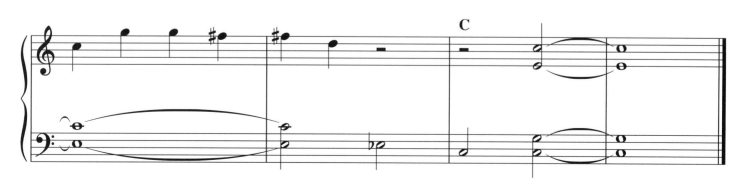

The Exodus Theme

from EXODUS

By Ernest Gold

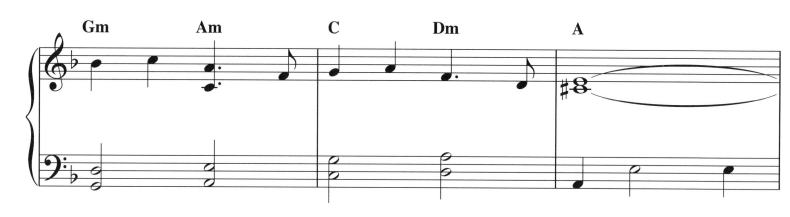

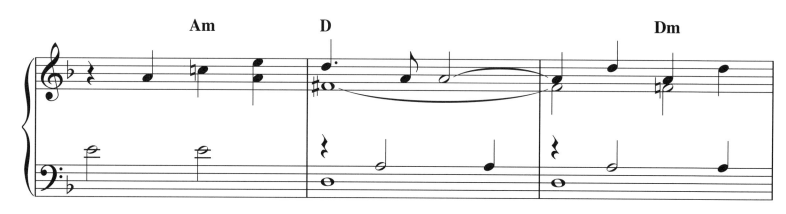

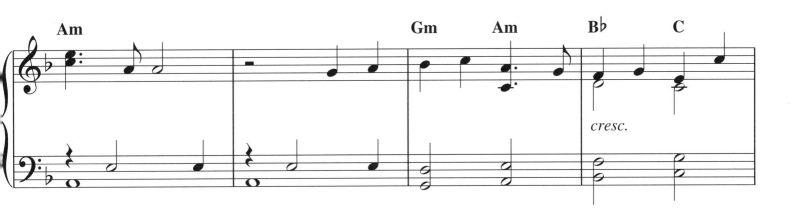

27

The Godfather

(Love Theme)
from the Paramount Picture THE GODFATHER

By Nino Rota

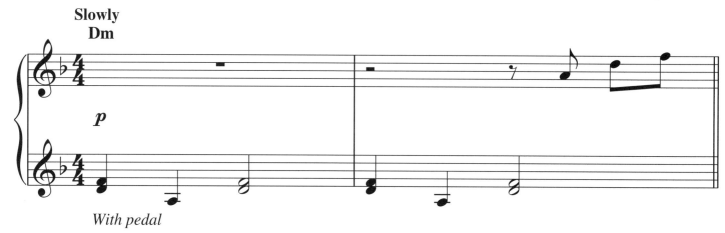

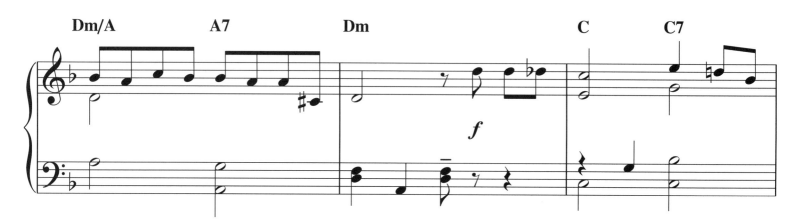

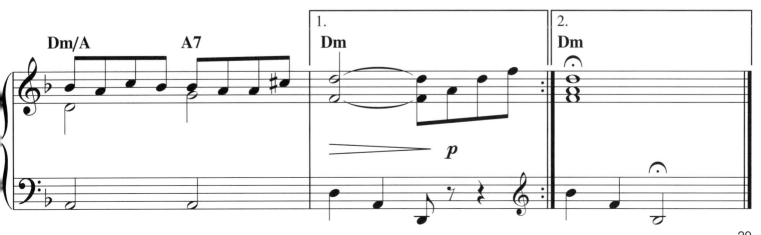

Love Story

Theme from the Paramount Picture LOVE STORY

Music by Francis Lai

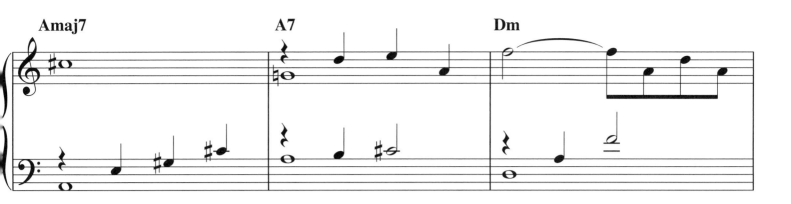

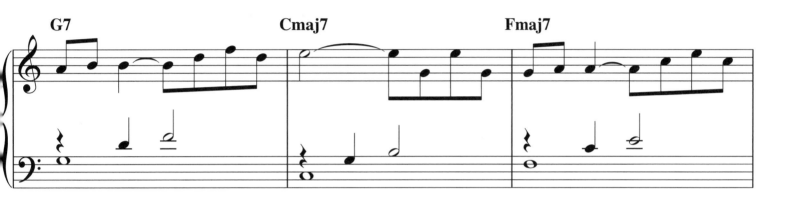

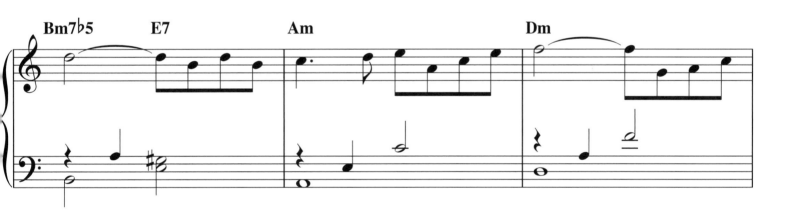

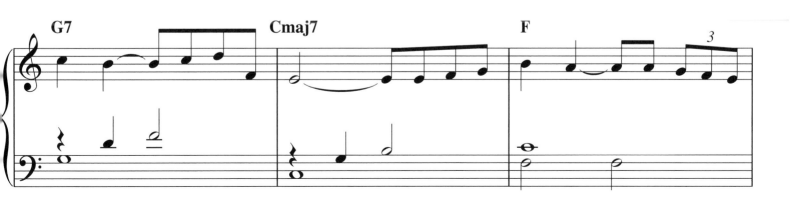

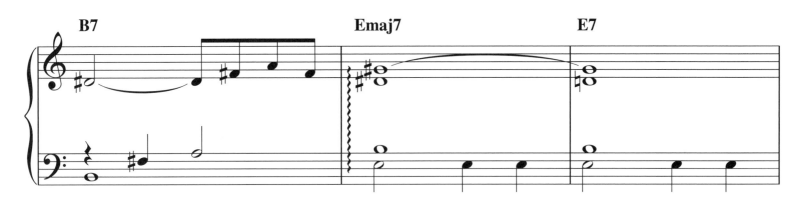

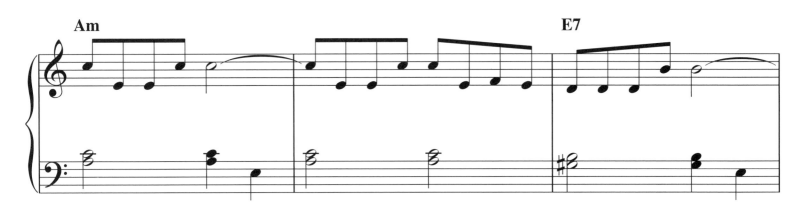

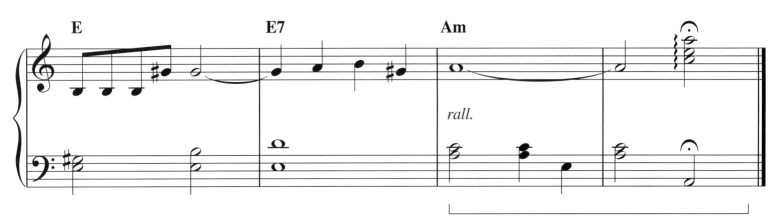

A Man and a Woman

(Un homme et une femme)

from A MAN AND A WOMAN

Original Words by Pierre Barouh
English Words by Jerry Keller

Music by Francis Lai

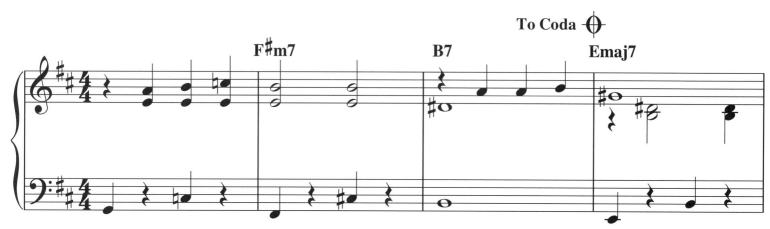

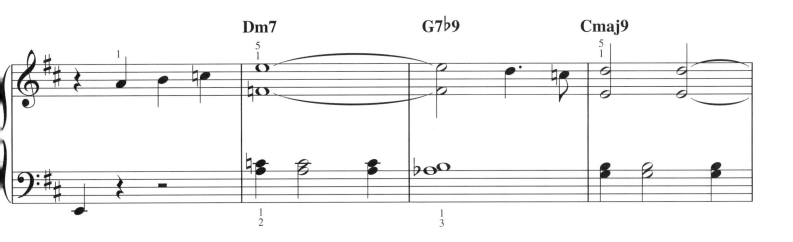

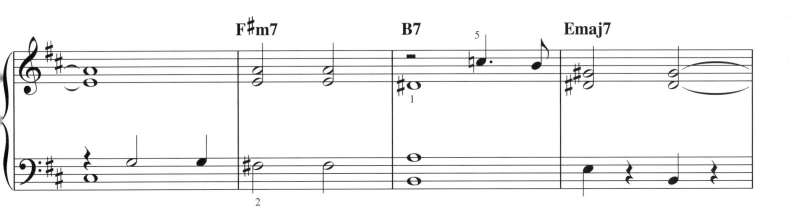

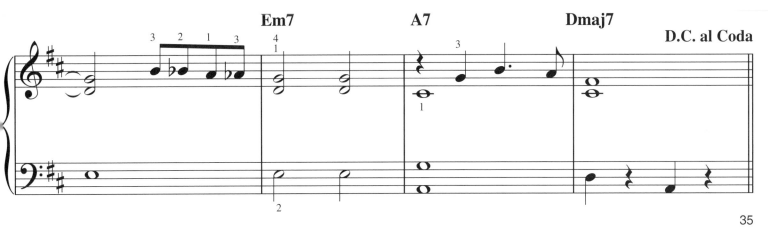

D.C. al Coda

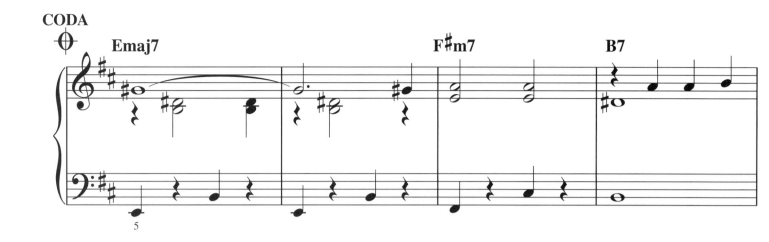

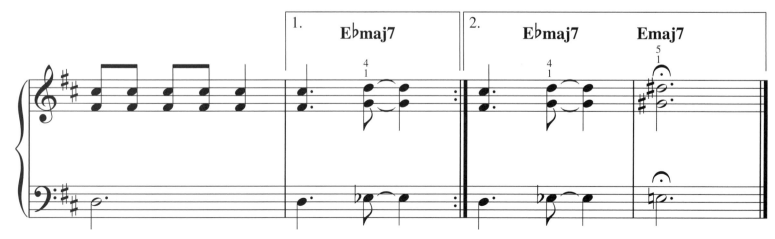

The March of the Siamese Children

from THE KING AND I

Music by Richard Rodgers

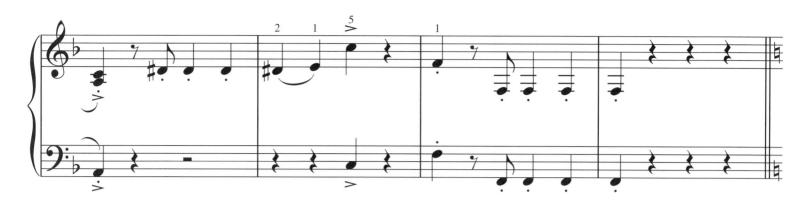

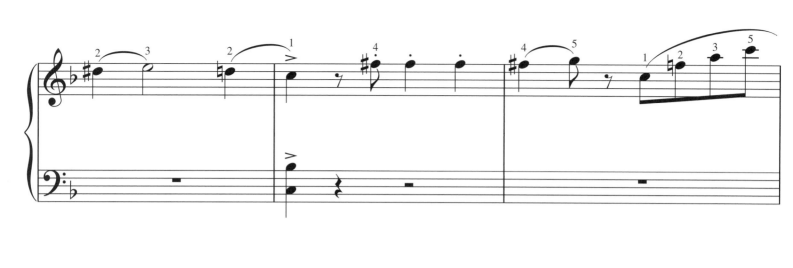

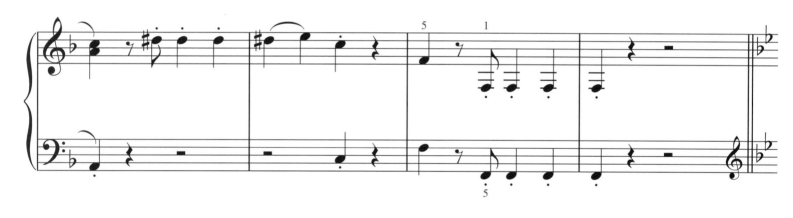

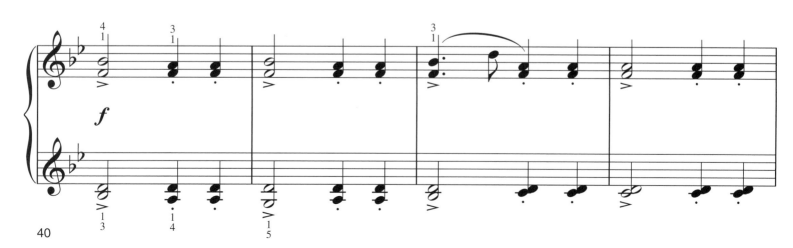

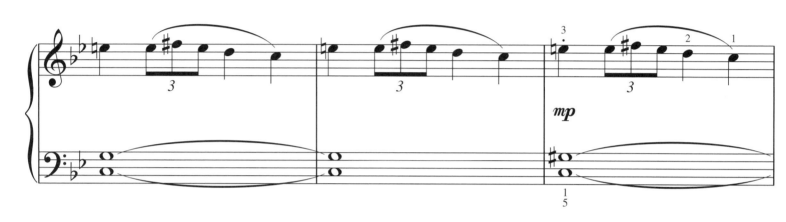

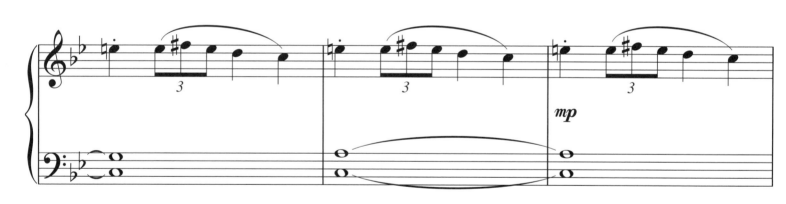

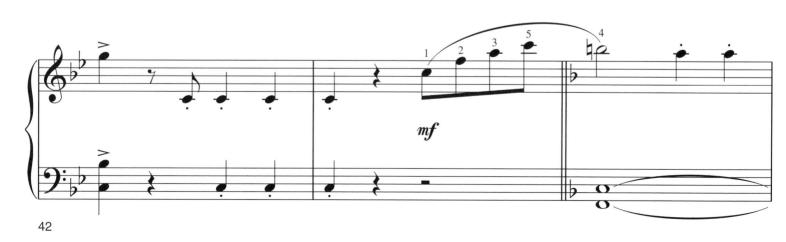

Midnight in Moscow

Based on a song by
Vassili Soloviev-Sedoy and M. Matusovsky
New Music by Kenny Ball

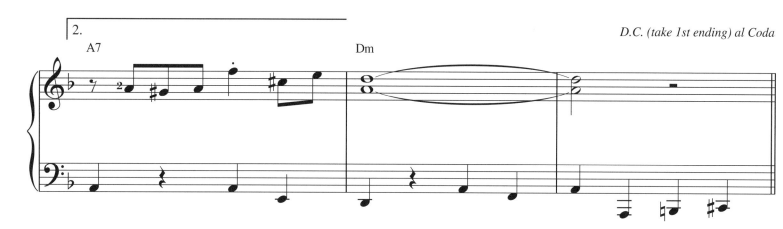

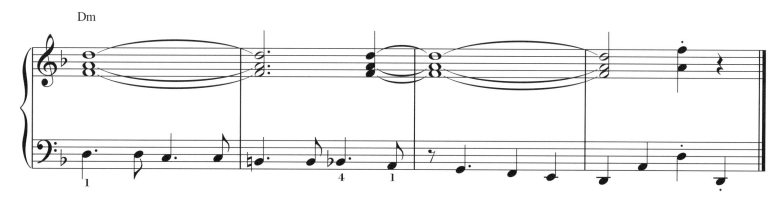

Music to Watch Girls By

By Sid Ramin

More
(Ti guarderò nel cuore)
from the Film MONDO CANE

Italian Lyrics by Marcello Ciorciolini
English Lyrics by Norman Newell

Music by
Nino Oliviero and Riz Ortolani

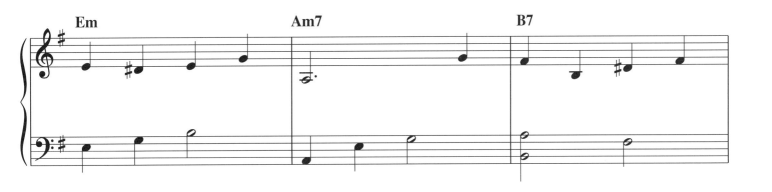

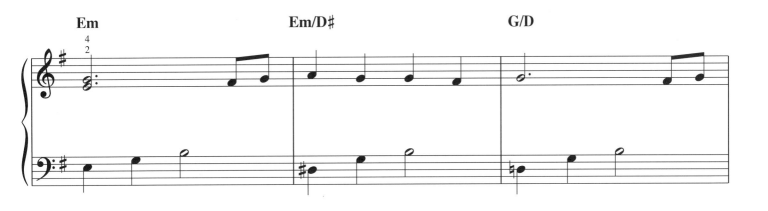

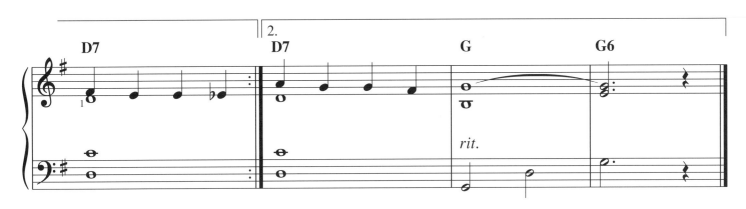

Peter Gunn

Theme Song from the Television Series

By Henry Mancini

Moderately

L.H. 8vb throughout

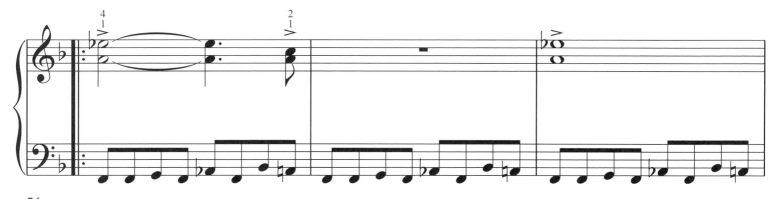

The Pink Panther

from THE PINK PANTHER

By Henry Mancini

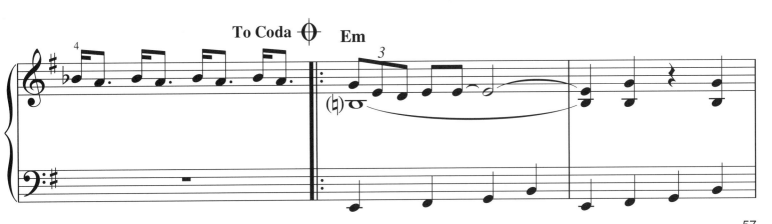

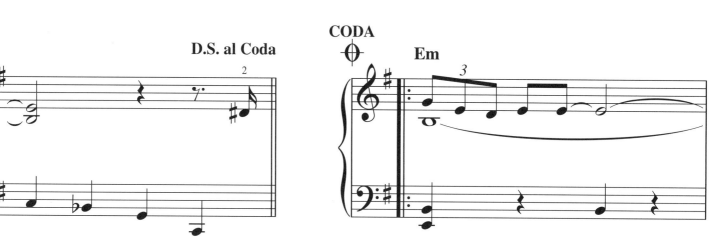

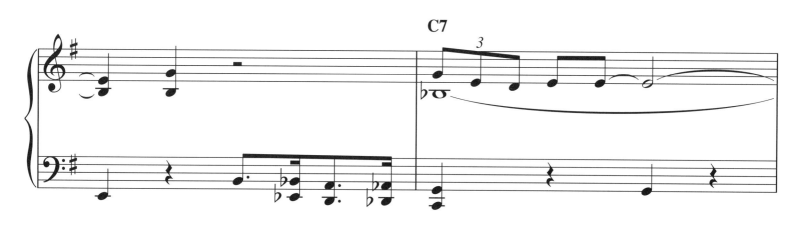

Romeo and Juliet

(Love Theme)

from the Paramount Picture ROMEO AND JULIET

By Nino Rota

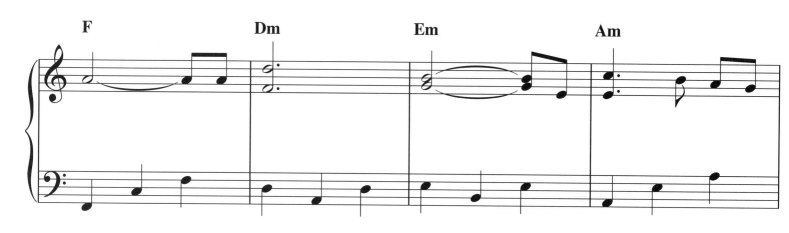

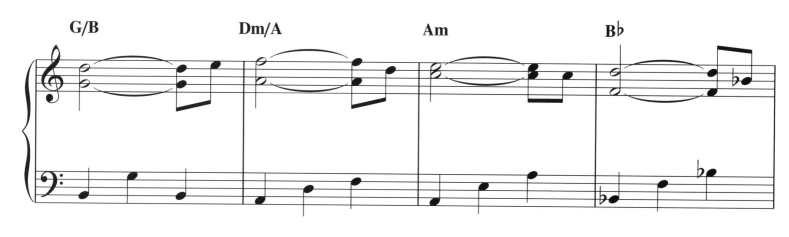

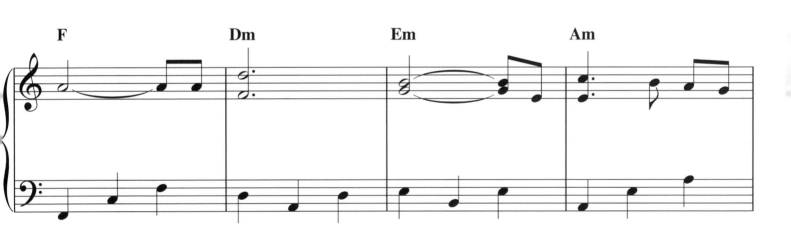

Love Theme from "St. Elmo's Fire"

from the Motion Picture ST. ELMO'S FIRE

Words and Music by
David Foster

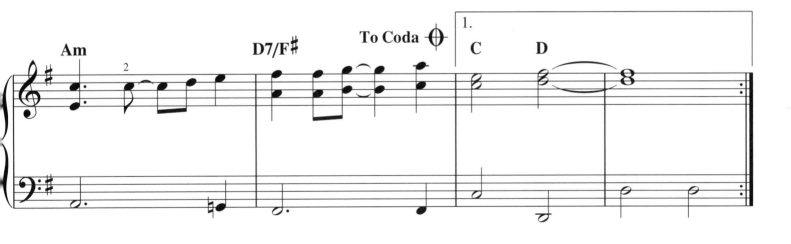

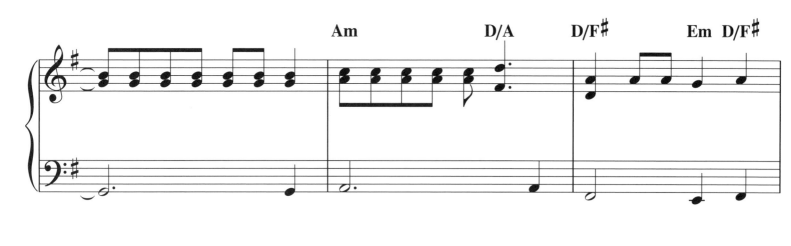

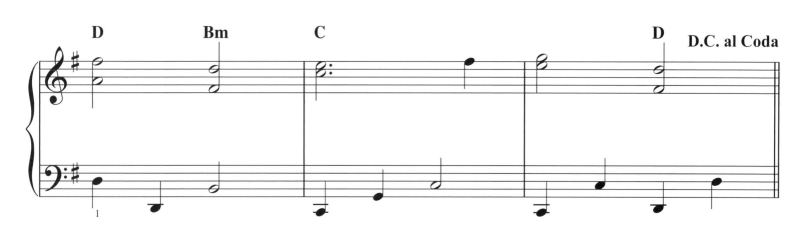

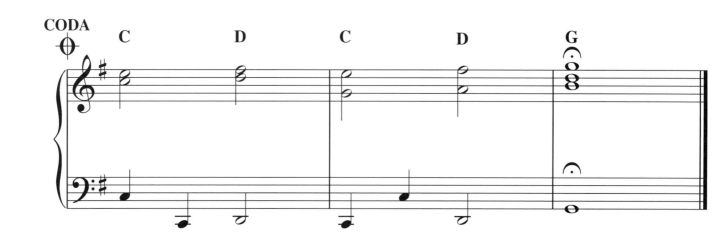

St. Elsewhere

from the Television Series ST. ELSEWHERE

By Dave Grusin

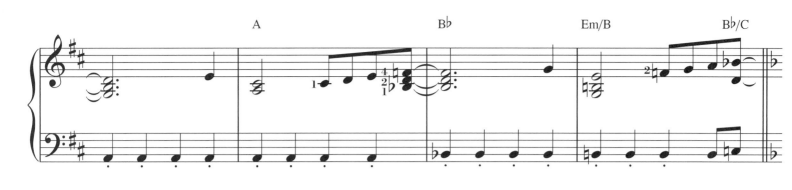

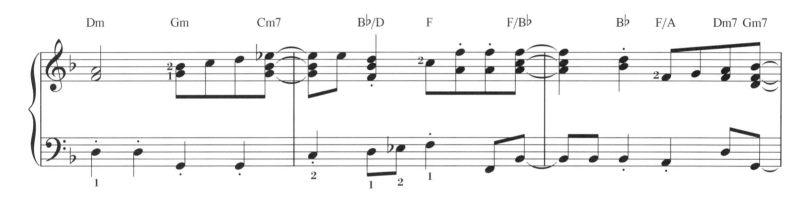

Sleepwalk

By Santo Farina,
John Farina and Ann Farina

Somewhere in My Memory

from the Twentieth Century Fox Motion Picture HOME ALONE

Words by Leslie Bricusse

Music by John Williams

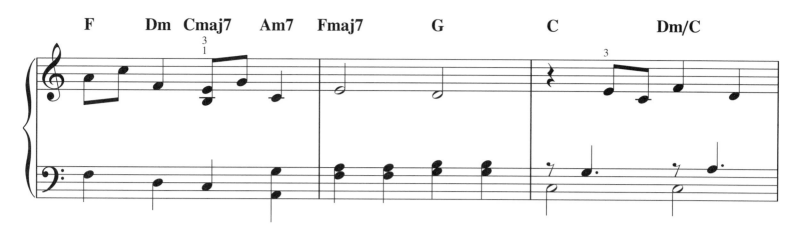

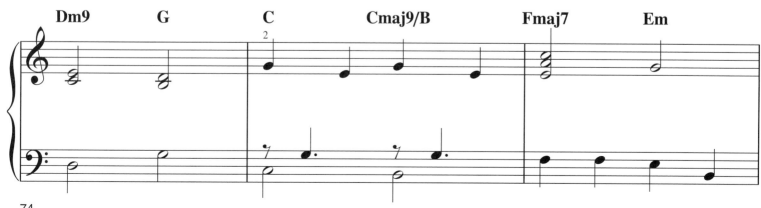

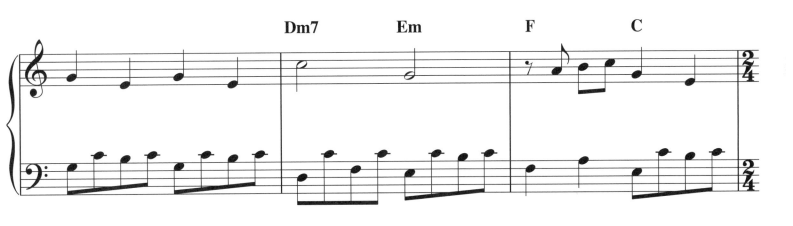

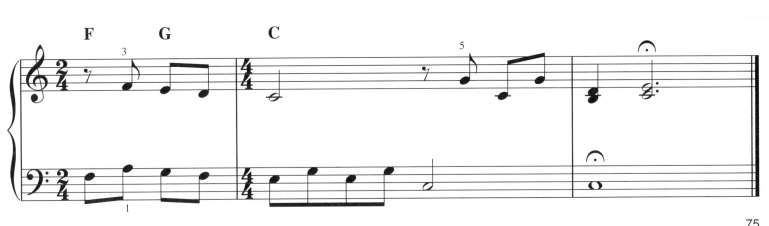

Stranger on the Shore

from FLAMINGO KID

Words by
Robert Mellin

Music by
Acker Bilk

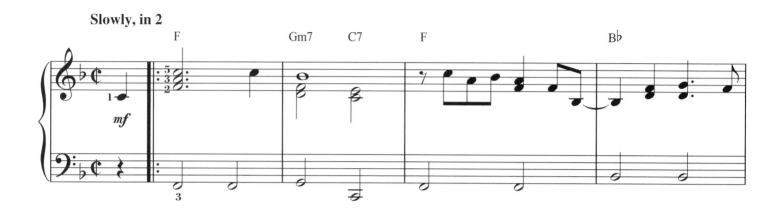

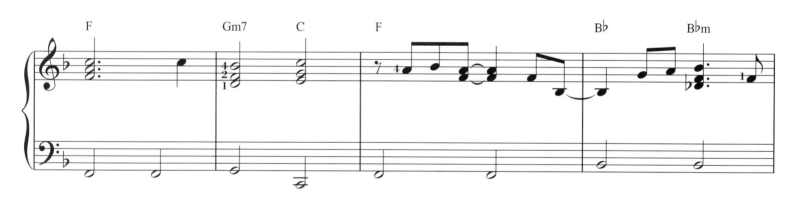

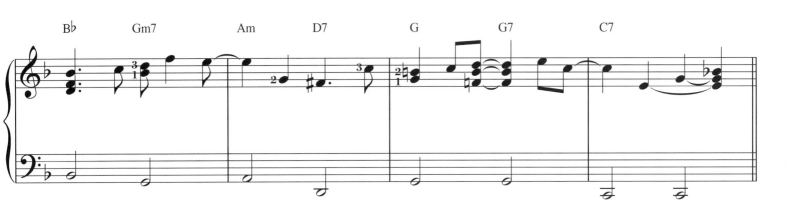

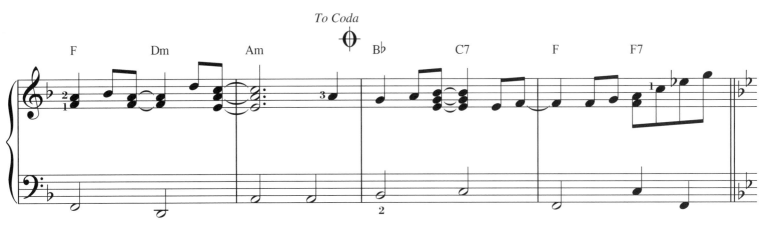

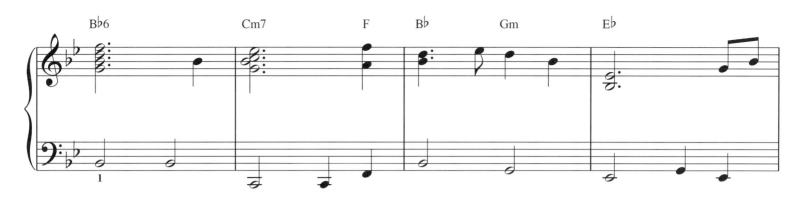

D.S. al Coda

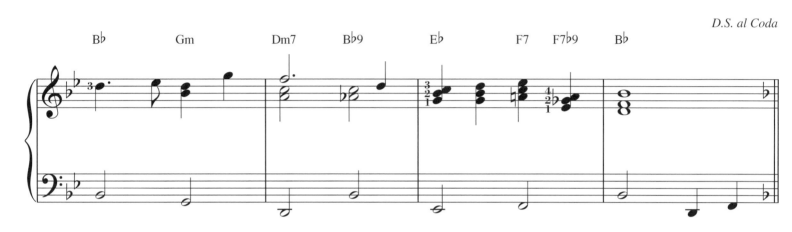

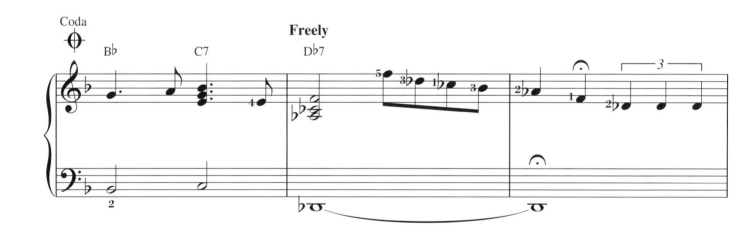

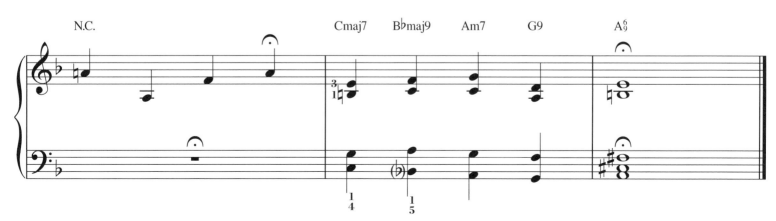

Theme from Summer of '42

(The Summer Knows)

Music by Michel Legrand

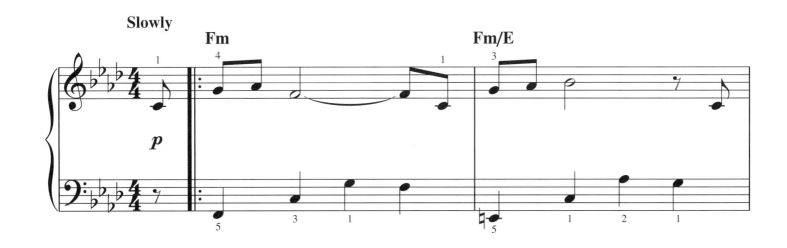

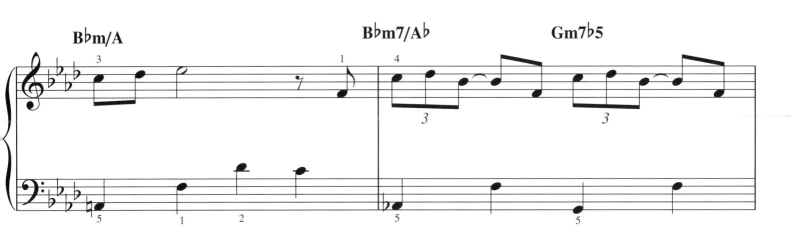

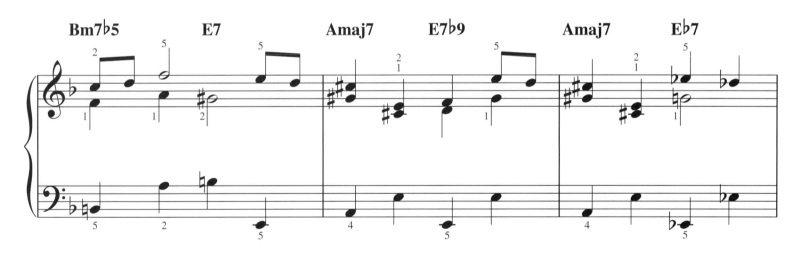

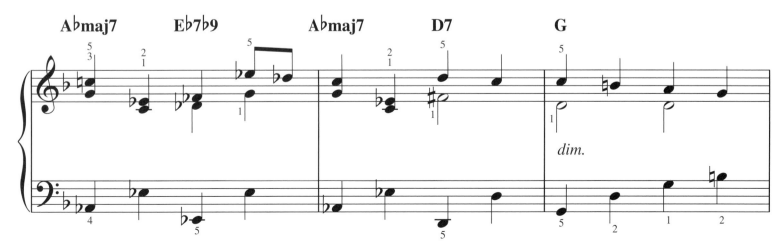

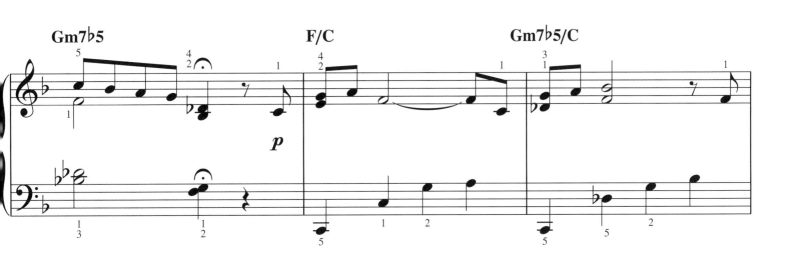

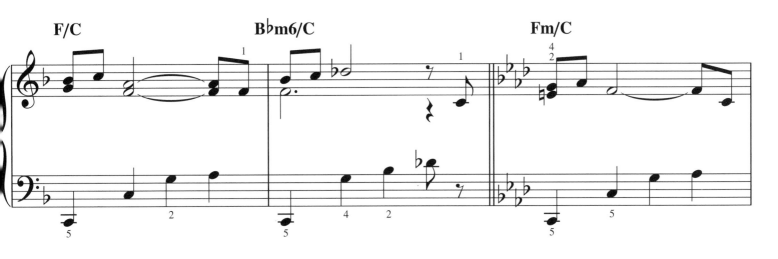

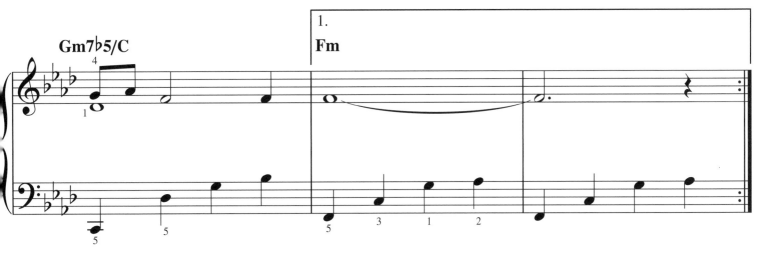

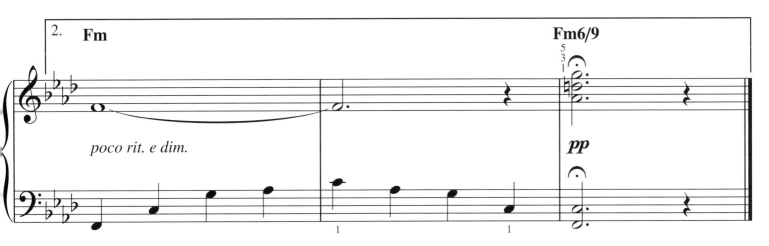

Tequila

By Chuck Rio

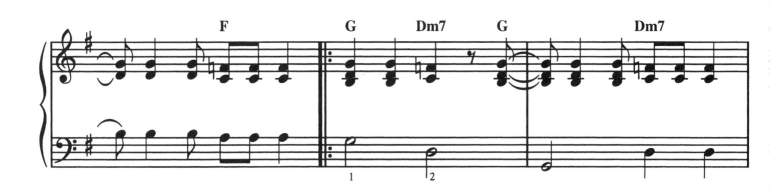

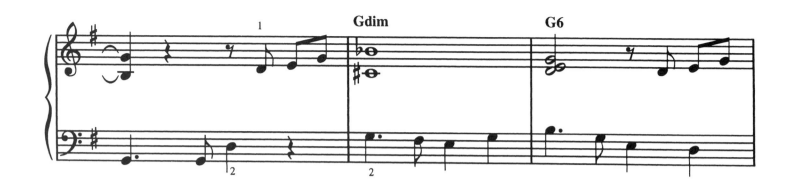

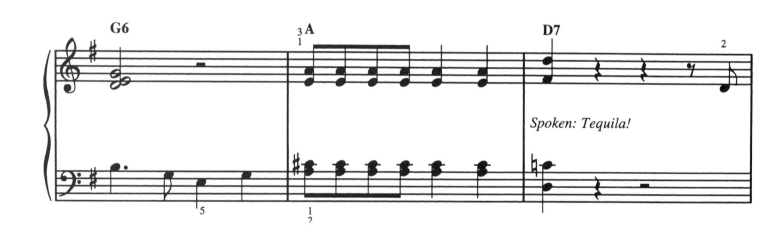

Spoken: Tequila!

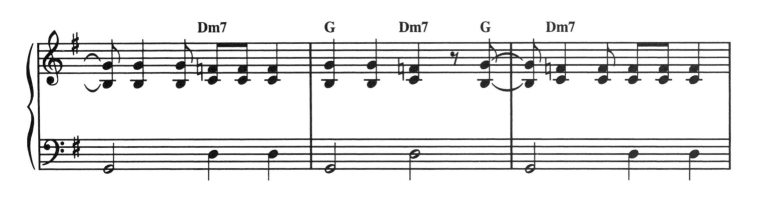

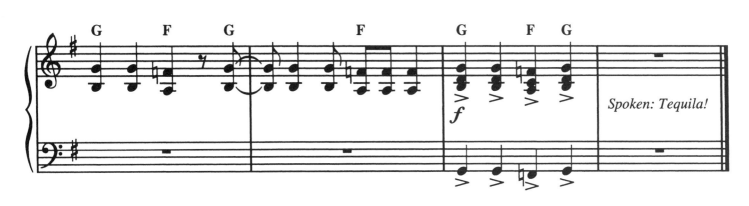

Wonderland by Night

Words by Lincoln Chase

Music by Klauss Gunter-Neuman

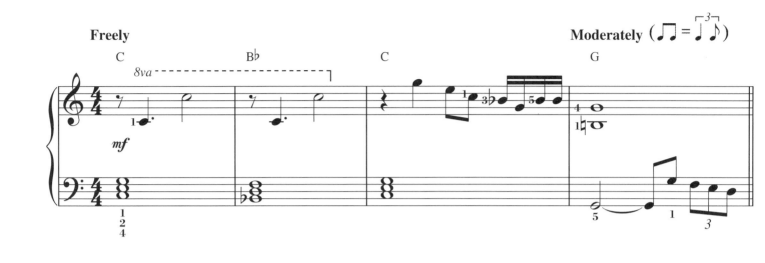

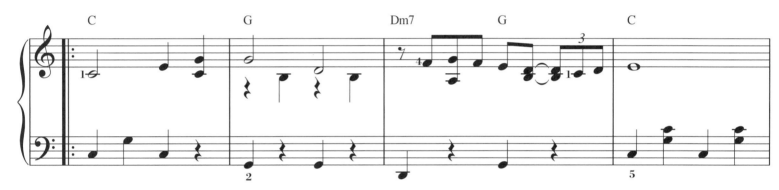

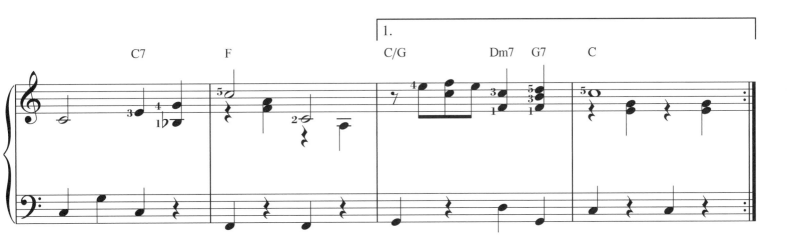

87

Tubular Bells

Theme from THE EXORCIST

By Mike Oldfield

Moderately fast

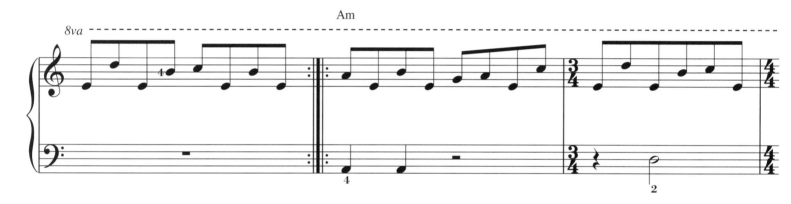

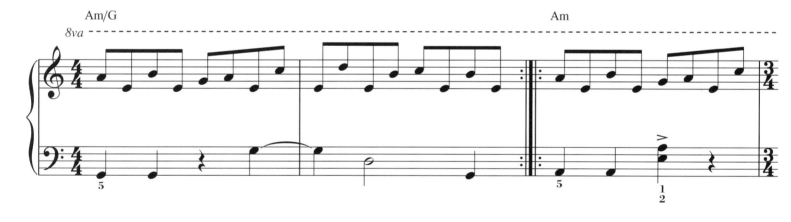

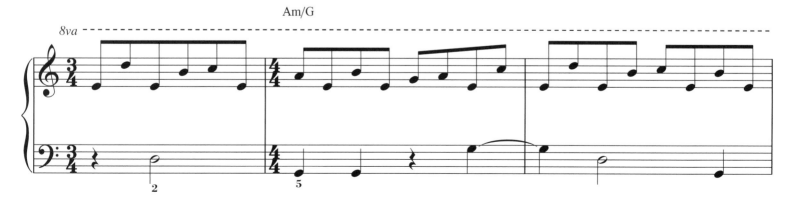

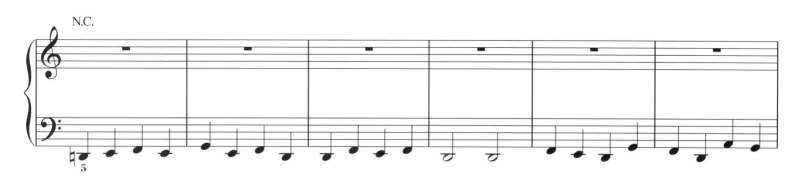

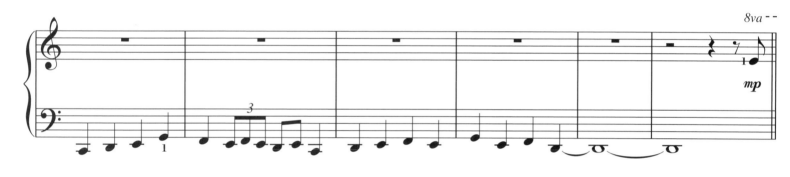

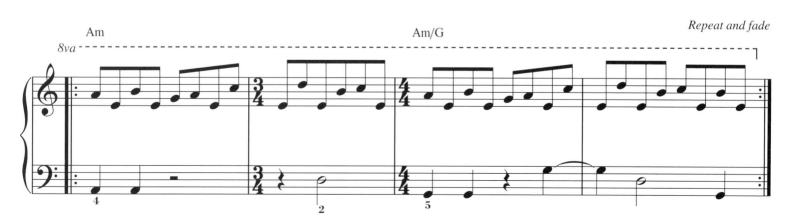

SUPPLY THE DEMAND
WITH THE MOST REQUESTED SERIES FROM

great songs series

This legendary series has delighted players and performers for generations.

Great Songs of Christmas
59 yuletide favorites in piano/vocal/guitar format, including: Breath of Heaven (Mary's Song) • Christmas Time Is Here • Frosty the Snow Man • I'll Be Home for Christmas • Jingle-Bell Rock • Nuttin' for Christmas • O Little Town of Bethlehem • Silver Bells • The Twelve Days of Christmas • What Child Is This? • and many more.
02501543 P/V/G................................$17.99

Great Songs of Country Music
This volume features 58 country gems, including: Abilene • Afternoon Delight • Amazed • Annie's Song • Blue • Crazy • Elvira • Fly Away • For the Good Times • Friends in Low Places • The Gambler • Hey, Good Lookin' • I Hope You Dance • Thank God I'm a Country Boy • This Kiss • Your Cheatin' Heart • and more.
02500503 P/V/G................................$19.95

Great Songs of Folk Music
Nearly 50 of the most popular folk songs of our time, including: Blowin' in the Wind • The House of the Rising Sun • Puff the Magic Dragon • This Land Is Your Land • Time in a Bottle • The Times They Are A-Changin' • The Unicorn • Where Have All the Flowers Gone? • and more.
02500997 P/V/G................................$19.95

Great Songs from The Great American Songbook
52 American classics, including: Ain't That a Kick in the Head • As Time Goes By • Come Fly with Me •Georgia on My Mind • I Get a Kick Out of You • I've Got You Under My Skin • The Lady Is a Tramp • Love and Marriage • Mack the Knife • Misty • Over the Rainbow • People • Take the "A" Train • Thanks for the Memory • and more.
02500760 P/V/G................................$16.95

Great Songs of the Movies
Nearly 60 of the best songs popularized in the movies, including: Accidentally in Love • Alfie • Almost Paradise • The Rainbow Connection • Somewhere in My Memory • Take My Breath Away (Love Theme) • Three Coins in the Fountain • (I've Had) the Time of My Life • Up Where We Belong • The Way We Were • and more.
02500967 P/V/G................................$19.95

Great Songs of the Pop Era
Over 50 hits from the pop era, including: Every Breath You Take • I'm Every Woman • Just the Two of Us • Leaving on a Jet Plane • My Cherie Amour • Raindrops Keep Fallin' on My Head • Time After Time • (I've Had) the Time of My Life • What a Wonderful World • and more.
02500043 Easy Piano..........................$16.95

Great Songs for Weddings
A beautiful collection of 59 pop standards perfect for wedding ceremonies and receptions, including: Always and Forever • Amazed • Beautiful in My Eyes • Can You Feel the Love Tonight • Endless Love • Love of a Lifetime • Open Arms • Unforgettable • When I Fall in Love • The Wind Beneath My Wings • and more.
02501006 P/V/G................................$19.95

Great Songs of the Fifties
Features rock, pop, country, Broadway and movie tunes, including: All Shook Up • At the Hop • Blue Suede Shoes • Dream Lover • Fly Me to the Moon • Kansas City • Love Me Tender • Misty • Peggy Sue • Rock Around the Clock • Sea of Love • Sixteen Tons • Take the "A" Train • Wonderful! Wonderful! • and more. Includes an introduction by award-winning journalist Bruce Pollock.
02500323 P/V/G................................$16.95

Great Songs of the Sixties, Vol. 1 – Revised
The updated version of this classic book includes 80 faves from the 1960s: Angel of the Morning • Bridge over Troubled Water • Cabaret • Different Drum • Do You Believe in Magic • Eve of Destruction • Monday, Monday • Spinning Wheel • Walk on By • and more.
02509902 P/V/G................................$19.95

Great Songs of the Sixties, Vol. 2 – Revised
61 more '60s hits: California Dreamin' • Crying • For Once in My Life • Honey • Little Green Apples • MacArthur Park • Me and Bobby McGee • Nowhere Man • Piece of My Heart • Sugar, Sugar • You Made Me So Very Happy • and more.
02509904 P/V/G................................$19.95

Great Songs of the Seventies, Vol. 1 – Revised
This super collection of 70 big hits from the '70s includes: After the Love Has Gone • Afternoon Delight • Annie's Song • Band on the Run • Cold as Ice • FM • Imagine • It's Too Late • Layla • Let It Be • Maggie May • Piano Man • Shelter from the Storm • Superstar • Sweet Baby James • Time in a Bottle • The Way We Were • and more.
02509917 P/V/G................................$19.95

Great Songs of the Eighties – Revised
This edition features 50 songs in rock, pop & country styles, plus hits from Broadway and the movies! Songs: Almost Paradise • Angel of the Morning • Do You Really Want to Hurt Me • Endless Love • Flashdance...What a Feeling • Guilty • Hungry Eyes • (Just Like) Starting Over • Let Love Rule • Missing You • Patience • Through the Years • Time After Time • Total Eclipse of the Heart • and more.
02502125 P/V/G................................$18.95

Great Songs of the Nineties
Includes: Achy Breaky Heart • Beautiful in My Eyes • Believe • Black Hole Sun • Black Velvet • Blaze of Glory • Building a Mystery • Crash into Me • Fields of Gold • From a Distance • Glycerine • Here and Now • Hold My Hand • I'll Make Love to You • Ironic • Linger • My Heart Will Go On • Waterfalls • Wonderwall • and more.
02500040 P/V/G................................$16.95

Great Songs of 2000-2009
Over 50 of the decade's biggest hits, including: Accidentally in Love • Breathe (2 AM) • Daughters • Hanging by a Moment • The Middle • The Remedy (I Won't Worry) • Smooth • A Thousand Miles • and more.
02500922 P/V/G................................$24.99

Great Songs of Broadway – Revised Edition
This updated edition is loaded with 54 hits: And All That Jazz • Be Italian • Comedy Tonight • Consider Yourself • Dulcinea • Edelweiss • Friendship • Getting to Know You • Hopelessly Devoted to You • If I Loved You • The Impossible Dream •Mame • On My Own • On the Street Where You Live • People • Try to Remember • Unusual Way • When You're Good to Mama • Where Is Love? • and more.
02501545 P/V/G................................$19.99

Great Songs for Children
90 wonderful, singable favorites kids love: Baa Baa Black Sheep • Bingo • The Candy Man • Do-Re-Mi • Eensy Weensy Spider • The Hokey Pokey • Linus and Lucy • Sing • This Old Man • Yellow Submarine • and more, with a touching foreword by Grammy-winning singer/songwriter Tom Chapin.
02501348 P/V/G................................$19.99

Prices, contents, and availability subject to change without notice.

Exclusively Distributed By
HAL•LEONARD CORPORATION
7777 W. Bluemound Rd. P.O. Box 13819 Milwaukee, WI 53213

www.cherrylane.com

0411

More Big-Note & Easy Piano Books

For a complete listing of Cherry Lane titles available, including contents listings, please visit our web site at www.cherrylane.

CHOPIN FOR EASY PIANO

This special easy piano version features the composer's intricate melodies, harmonies and rhythms newly arranged so that virtually all pianists can experience the thrill of playing Chopin at the piano! Includes 20 favorites mazurkas, nocturnes, polonaises, preludes and waltzes.
_____02501483 Easy Piano...............$7.99

CLASSICAL CHRISTMAS

Easy solo arrangements of 30 wonderful holiday songs: Ave Maria • Dance of the Sugar Plum Fairy • Evening Prayer • Gesu Bambino • Hallelujah! • He Shall Feed His Flock • March of the Toys • O Come, All Ye Faithful • O Holy Night • Pastoral Symphony • Sheep May Safely Graze • Sinfonia • Waltz of the Flowers • and more.
_____02500112 Easy Piano Solo.......$9.95

BEST OF JOHN DENVER

A collection of 18 Denver classics, including: Leaving on a Jet Plane • Take Me Home, Country Roads • Rocky Mountain High • Follow Me • and more.
_____02505512 Easy Piano...............$9.95

JOHN DENVER ANTHOLOGY

Easy arrangements of 34 of the finest from this beloved artist. Includes: Annie's Song • Fly Away • Follow Me • Grandma's Feather Bed • Leaving on a Jet Plane • Perhaps Love • Rocky Mountain High • Sunshine on My Shoulders • Take Me Home, Country Roads • Thank God I'm a Country Boy • and many more.
_____02501366 Easy Piano.............$19.99

EASY BROADWAY SHOWSTOPPERS

Easy piano arrangements of 16 traditional and new Broadway standards, including: "Impossible Dream" from *Man of La Mancha* • "Unusual Way" from *Nine* • "This Is the Moment" from *Jekyll & Hyde* • many more.
_____02505517 Easy Piano.............$12.95

A FAMILY CHRISTMAS AROUND THE PIANO

25 songs for hours of family fun, including: Away in a Manger • Deck the Hall • The First Noel • God Rest Ye Merry, Gentlemen • Hark! the Herald Angels Sing • Jingle Bells • Jolly Old St. Nicholas • Joy to the World • O Little Town of Bethlehem • Silent Night, Holy Night • The Twelve Days of Christmas • and more.
_____02500398 Easy Piano...............$8.99

FAVORITE CELTIC SONGS FOR EASY PIANO

Easy arrangements of 40 Celtic classics, including: The Ash Grove • The Bluebells of Scotland • A Bunch of Thyme • Danny Boy • Finnegan's Wake • I'll Tell Me Ma • Loch Lomond • My Wild Irish Rose • The Rose of Tralee • and more!
_____02501306 Easy Piano.............$12.99

FAVORITE POP BALLADS

This new collection features 35 beloved ballads, including: Breathe (2 AM) • Faithfully • Leaving on a Jet Plane • Open Arms • Ordinary People • Summer Breeze • These Eyes • Truly • You've Got a Friend • and more.
_____02501005 Easy Piano.............$15.99

HOLY CHRISTMAS CAROLS COLORING BOOK

A terrific songbook with 7 sacred carols and lots of coloring pages for the young pianist. Songs include: Angels We Have Heard on High • The First Noel • Hark! The Herald Angels Sing • It Came upon a Midnight Clear • O Come All Ye Faithful • O Little Town of Bethlehem • Silent Night.
_____02500277 Five-Finger Piano $6.95

JEKYLL & HYDE – VOCAL SELECTIONS

Ten songs from the Wildhorn/Bricusse Broadway smash, arranged for big-note: In His Eyes • It's a Dangerous Game • Lost in the Darkness • A New Life • No One Knows Who I Am • Once Upon a Dream • Someone Like You • Sympathy, Tenderness • Take Me as I Am • This Is the Moment.
_____02500023 Big-Note Piano........$9.95

JACK JOHNSON ANTHOLOGY

Easy arrangements of 27 of the best from this Hawaiian singer/songwriter, including: Better Together • Breakdown • Flake • Fortunate Fool • Good People • Sitting, Waiting, Wishing • Taylor • and more.
_____02501313 Easy Piano.............$19.99

JUST FOR KIDS – NOT! CHRISTMAS SONGS

This unique collection of 14 Christmas favorites is fun for the whole family! Kids can play the full-sounding big-note solos alone, or with their parents (or teachers) playing accompaniment for the thrill of four-hand piano! Includes: Deck the Halls • Jingle Bells • Silent Night • What Child Is This? • and more.
_____02505510 Big-Note Piano........$8.95

JUST FOR KIDS – NOT! CLASSICS

Features big-note arrangements of classical masterpieces, plus optional accompaniment for adults. Songs: Air on the G String • Dance of the Sugar Plum Fairy • Für Elise • Jesu, Joy of Man's Desiring • Ode to Joy • Pomp and Circumstance • The Sorcerer's Apprentice • William Tell Overture • and more!
_____02505513 Classics $7.95
_____02500301 More Classics..........$8.95

JUST FOR KIDS – NOT! FUN SONGS

Fun favorites for kids everywhere in big-note arrangements for piano, including: Bingo • Eensy Weensy Spider • Farmer in the Dell • Jingle Bells • London Bridge • Pop Goes the Weasel • Puff the Magic Dragon • Skip to My Lou • Twinkle, Twinkle Little Star • and more!
_____02505523 Fun Songs $7.95

JUST FOR KIDS – NOT! TV THEMES & MOVIE SONGS

Entice the kids to the piano with this delightful collection of songs and themes from movies and TV. These big-note arrangements include themes from The Brady Bunch and The Addams Family, as well as Do-Re-Mi (The Sound of Music), theme from Beetlejuice (Day-O) and Puff the Magic Dragon. Each song includes an accompaniment part for teacher or adult so that the kids can experience the joy of four-hand playing as well! Plus performance tips.
_____02505507 TV Themes & Movie Songs.....................$9.95
_____02500304 More TV Themes & Movie Songs.....................$9.95

MERRY CHRISTMAS, EVERYONE

Over 20 contemporary and classic all-time holiday favorites arranged for big-note piano or easy piano. Includes: Away in a Manger • Christmas Like a Lullaby • The First Noel • Joy to the World • The Marvelous Toy • and more.
_____02505600 Big-Note Piano........$9.95

POKEMON 2 B.A. MASTER

This great songbook features easy piano arrangements of 13 tunes from the hit TV series: 2.B.A. Master • Double Trouble (Team Rocket) • Everything Changes • Misty's Song • My Best Friends • Pokémon (Dance Mix) • Pokémon Theme • PokéRAP • The Time Has Come (Pikachu's Goodbye) • Together, Forever • Viridian City • What Kind of Pokémon Are You? • You Can Do It (If You Really Try). Includes a full-color, 8-page pull-out section featuring characters and scenes from this super hot show.
_____02500145 Easy Piano.............$12.95

POP/ROCK LOVE SONGS

Easy arrangements of 18 romatic favorites, including: Always • Bed of Roses • Butterfly Kisses • Follow Me • From This Moment On • Hard Habit to Break • Leaving on a Jet Plane • When You Say Nothing at All • more.
_____02500151 Easy Piano.............$10.95

POPULAR CHRISTMAS CAROLS COLORING BOOK

Kids are sure to love this fun holiday songbook! It features five-finger piano arrangements of seven Christmas classics, complete with coloring pages throughout! Songs include: Deck the Hall • Good King Wenceslas • Jingle Bells • Jolly Old St. Nicholas • O Christmas Tree • Up on the Housetop • We Wish You a Merry Christmas.
_____02500276 Five-Finger Piano $6.95

PUFF THE MAGIC DRAGON & 54 OTHER ALL-TIME CHILDREN'S FAVORITESONGS

55 timeless songs enjoyed by generations of kids, and sure to be favorites for years to come. Songs include: A-Tisket A-Tasket • Alouette • Eensy Weensy Spider • The Farmer in the Dell • I've Been Working on the Railroad • If You're Happy and You Know It • Joy to the World • Michael Finnegan • Oh Where, Oh Where Has My Little Dog Gone • Silent Night • Skip to My Lou • This Old Man • and many more.
_____02500017 Big-Note Piano $12.95

See your local music dealer or contact:

EXCLUSIVELY DISTRIBUTED BY
HAL•LEONARD®
7777 W. BLUEMOUND RD. P.O. BOX 13819 MILWAUKEE, WI 53213

Prices, contents, and availability subject to change without notice.

More Great Piano/Vocal Books

FROM CHERRY LANE

For a complete listing of Cherry Lane titles available,
including contents listings, please visit our web site at

www.cherrylane.com

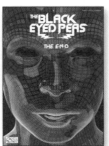

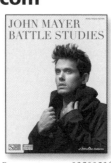

See your local music dealer or contact:

EXCLUSIVELY DISTRIBUTED BY
HAL•LEONARD®
CORPORATION
7777 W. BLUEMOUND RD. P.O. BOX 13819 MILWAUKEE, WI 53213

Prices, contents and availability subject to change without notice.

0811